CATS AND DOGS
and Other Pets

Peter Gray

FRANKLIN WATTS

First published in 2013 by Franklin Watts

Copyright © 2013 Arcturus Publishing Limited

Franklin Watts
338 Euston Road
London NW1 3BH

Franklin Watts Australia
Level 17/207 Kent Street, Sydney NSW 2000

Produced by Arcturus Publishing Limited,
26/27 Bickels Yard, 151–153 Bermondsey Street, London SE1 3HA

Illustrations: © Peter Gray
Editors: Joe Harris and Nicola Barber
Design: sprout.uk.com
Cover design: sprout.uk.com

A CIP catalogue record for this book is available from the British Library.

Dewey Decimal Classification Number 743.6

ISBN 978 1 4451 1875 8

Printed in China

Franklin Watts is a division of Hachette Children's Books, an Hachette UK company.
www.hachette.co.uk

SL002686EN

Supplier 03, Date 0513, Print Run 2383

CONTENTS

DRAWING

Start your drawings with simple guidelines before fleshing them out with detail.

Build up the general shape of your subject with guidelines. I have drawn the guidelines quite heavily to make them easy to follow, but you should work faintly with a hard pencil.

Guidelines

Use a softer pencil to develop the character and details. You may find that you do not follow the guidelines exactly in places. That's fine – they are only a rough guide.

Detail

Carefully erase the guidelines and mistakes. Then add shading and texture with a soft pencil.

Shading and texture

INKING

For a bold look, go over the outlines with ink. Wait for the ink to dry thoroughly, then erase all the pencil marks.

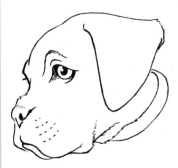

The easiest inking method is to use a felt-tip pen. If you plan to add paint at a later stage, make sure your pen is waterproof.

Felt-tip pen outlines

For a more graceful effect, use a fine-tipped watercolour brush dipped in ink.

Brush outlines

COLOURING

Although I use watercolours in this book, the main principles are the same for any materials – start with the shading, then add in markings and textures, and finally work your main colours over the top.

Felt-tip colouring

Felt-tip pens produce bright, vibrant colours. Work quickly to avoid the pen strokes remaining visible.

Coloured pencils

Coloured pencils are the easiest colouring tools to use, but you have to take great care to blend the colours to achieve a good finish.

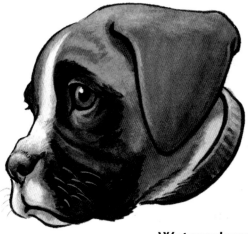

Watercolours

The subtlest effects can be achieved with watercolour paints. It is best to buy these as a set of solid blocks that you wet with a brush. Mix the colours in a palette or on an old white plate.

PAWS AND CLAWS

Just as many people find it difficult to draw human hands, a lot of us find it hard to draw animal paws. Here are some tips to make paws easy!

Here's a dog's paw seen from the side. Note that it is L-shaped and that the knuckles rise up slightly. The view of the bones inside will help you to understand the structure.

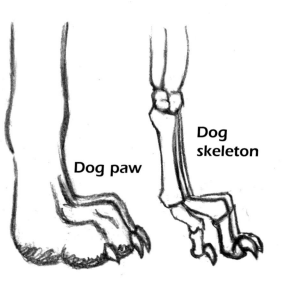

Dog paw

Dog skeleton

DRAWING PAWS

Dog and cat paws differ in the size of the claws and the general character – rounded for the cat and more **angular** for the dog.

For the guidelines, the main thing to consider is the overall shape of the paw.

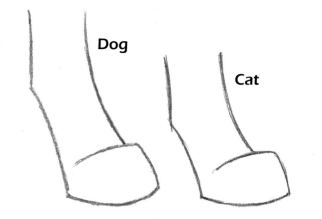

Dog

Cat

Divide the foot into toes. The middle two toes are much taller and broader than the outer ones.

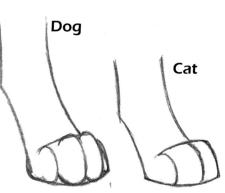

Dog

Cat

These examples are of short-haired breeds, so you can clearly see the shapes of the knuckles and the claws.

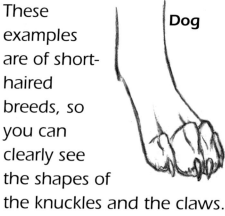

Dog

Cat

DRAWING FUR

Whether drawing a long- or short-haired animal, you can never show every hair – instead you need to simplify and suggest the texture of the fur. Generally, the more marks you use, the scruffier the animal will look.

Short fur detail

Long fur detail

Once the basic outline is right you can start to add details for the fur. The fur over the top of the head is usually shorter than that under the chin, and the fluffiest hairs are often found in the ears. Indicate the direction in which the fur flows over the body with simple marks.

Short fur

Long fur

The important thing to start with is to make the animal convincing before going into any detail. Where fur is very long, it can be sketched in as a broad shape.

Short fur inking

Long fur inking

To ink in the marks, use long, swift flowing strokes of the brush or pen and work around the whole drawing quickly. Don't feel that you need to ink every mark or outline – if the fur is very fine or pale, it will need no more than a few wispy strokes.

Golden retriever dogs are well-loved pets in many homes. They are gentle, loyal and very intelligent. They also love playing in water! Their thick golden coat has two different types of fur – a soft underneath layer that helps to keep the dog warm, and a shaggier outer layer that is water-resistant to keep the dog dry.

1 Dogs come in all shapes and sizes, but the first steps for drawing them are quite similar – it's just the **proportions** that change. The golden retriever has quite a large, long body with a relatively small head. Draw the body and head as simple shapes, an oval and a circle, with a space in between.

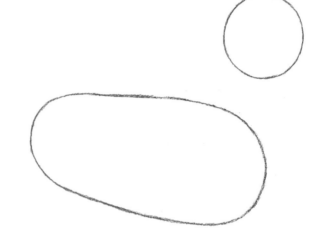

2 Now join the head to the body with curving lines that show the neck leaning forwards. Draw the upper part of the rear leg as a broad shape that also forms the dog's **rump**. Then mark the front edges of the legs, taking care to make them the right length.

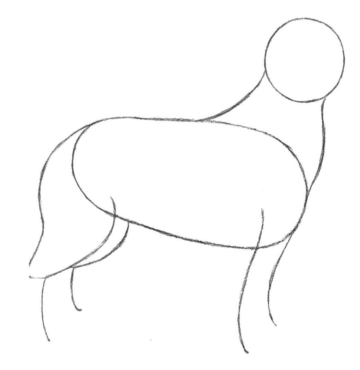

3 Finish the leg guidelines and add paw shapes. The tail is broad, curving to a point. Draw a roughly triangular **muzzle** and mark a centre line that curves over the top of the head. This will help you to position the eyes on either side of the line, and the ears on the sides of the head.

4 Add more detail to the face and draw some individual toes on each paw. Now start work on the coat. Show the shagginess of the coat with simple outlines and curving marks around the neck to suggest the direction of growth.

5 With all the guidelines in place you can now refine the drawing with a sharp pencil. Work on the face, aiming for a friendly expression. Add some more detail to the coat, mainly on the underside of the animal, behind the legs and around the neck and chest.

 6 To bring out the golden retriever's colouring, I used a pale yellow-brown ink for most of the outlining. I used black for the dark eyes, nose and mouth. Then I watered down some black ink to add detail to the paws and shadow areas.

7 For the shading I mixed some purple with dark yellow paint. I shaded the parts of the dog that would be in shadow with the light coming from the upper left. I also used this paint for some deep shadows in the coat, making sure my brush strokes followed the growth of the fur.

CLEVER DOGS

Golden retrievers are too friendly to be good guard dogs! But their intelligence means they can be trained to do many useful jobs for humans. These include working as guide dogs for blind people, or sniffing out people trapped after natural disasters such as earthquakes. Because they are such good swimmers, golden retrievers are also used for water rescues and life-saving!

ANIMAL FACTS

The colouring of most animals is not the same all over, and the golden retriever is no exception. Its colouring is richer along the back, the legs and parts of the head – generally where the coat is least fluffy. I painted these parts first with orange mixed into dark yellow, then softened the edges with a dampened tissue before the paint dried.

 To tie all the colours together I used a watery yellow-brown mix to wash over the entire dog.

 **10** For the finishing touches I added a few more spots of purple shade under the neck, inside the legs and on the paws. Then I used diluted white ink to paint on some highlights to make the fur shiny, and to bring out the features of the face and paws.

CAT

Cats have strong, flexible bodies. They walk lightly on their toes, and they are very agile and quick-footed. Like wild cats such as lions and tigers, many pet cats are hunters. They often catch their prey after dark, helped by their excellent night vision.

1 The view I have chosen shows the cat looking over its shoulder, so the circle that forms the head is placed almost centrally above the larger oval shape of the body. Make sure you leave a gap between the two shapes.

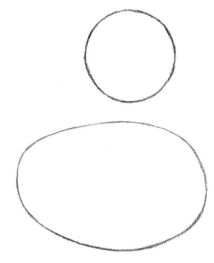

2 Join the two shapes with a long, arching neck line on the outer edge. For the front leg continue the neck line down, curving inwards. At the rear end form the shape of the upper leg and rump, then draw the leg shapes in between. The front legs should be wider than the rear.

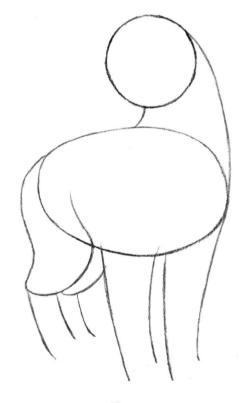

CAT TONGUES

Pet cats spend many hours each day grooming – licking their coats to keep them clean. Their tongues are rather like mini-hairbrushes! The surface of the tongue is covered with tiny, backwards-facing spines, which clean and untangle the fur as the cat licks.

ANIMAL FACTS

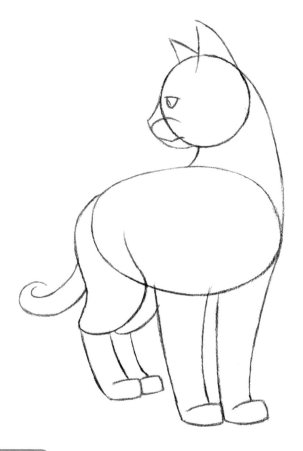

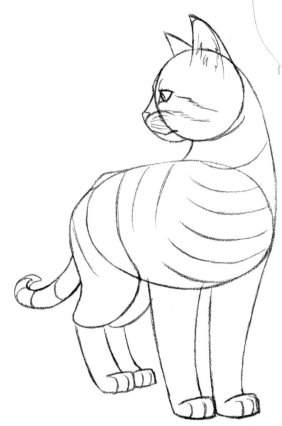

 3 Add the ears and the basic lines of the face and suddenly your drawing looks like a cat. Some feet shapes and a low-slung tail complete the basic outline.

4 Now put in some shaping and markings to the head and toes on the paws. Draw lines around the cat's body to guide you for the fur markings.

5 As you add detail to the drawing, pay attention to the shapes of the shoulders and hips. Make the outlines furry as you go. Draw character into the face and head, and put some striped markings across the body.

6 For the inking stage, I used a fine brush and black ink to create a furry texture with many fine strokes. I did not erase the pencil drawing because I wanted to follow the guidelines for the stripes at the next (painting) stage.

7 After painting the stripes in dark brown, I erased the pencil work. Then I added some orangey colour to the legs and feet. Once dry, I painted on some shadow in purpley-grey, then I washed blue-grey over the whole body. I used the same blue-grey to paint textural marks to give a rough, shaggy look. Then with watered-down white ink I brought out more of the shaggy texture as well as the highlights in the eyes, ear hairs and whiskers.

HAMSTER

Hamsters are **rodents** that live in the wild in many parts of the world, but which are also kept as pets. They are stout, short-tailed creatures that dig underground burrows and come out mainly at night.

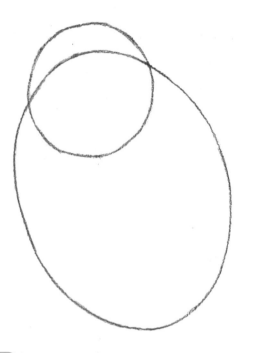

 Hamsters may look like balls of fluff, but they are not quite that simple to draw! This hamster picture starts with a large rounded oval overlapped by a circle at the top.

2 Mark guidelines on the head to show the centre and eye line. Then mark a centre line curving round the body with lines branching off down the length of the belly.

CHEEK POUCHES

Hamsters are excellent diggers and they build burrows with many tunnels and holes. They leave their burrows after dark to collect food, including grains, fruit, roots and insects. To transport it back to the burrow, they stuff the food into expandable cheek pouches on either sides of their head!

ANIMAL FACTS

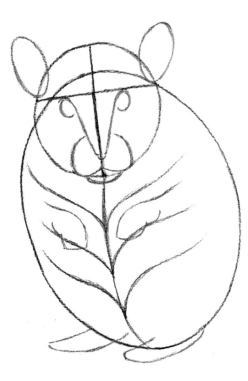

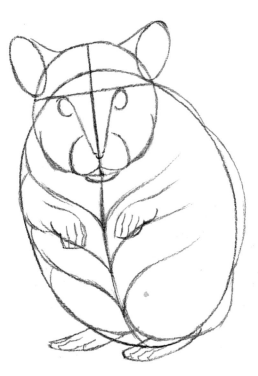

 Now add the basic shapes of the feet and hands. Place the eyes on the face just below the eye line, and the ears just above it. As you form the nose and mouth parts, work either side of the centre line to keep the features **symmetrical**.

 Add in toes and fingers. Continue to work on the overall shape of the hamster, curving the outline around the rolls of fat on the left-hand side and making it bulge out around the back and shoulders.

 Sharpen up the detail by adding some furry texture to the drawing. Make sure you have all the detail you need before going on to the inking stage.

 I used black ink for the darker parts of the outlines, the eyes, the back and deep shadows, and light brown for the paler parts. Try to keep all the ink lines short and hairy in texture.

7 For the colouring I mixed up a rich orange-brown. I left the underparts white and used purpley-grey for the shadow colour. I used pale pink on the hands, feet, nose and ears, where there is no fur. I also kept the brightest highlights for these parts.

RABBIT

The rabbit's most noticeable features are its long ears. It also has large, powerful back legs which it uses to hop – and to run very fast when necessary. Pet rabbits are often kept in hutches, but some are trained to live freely in people's homes as 'house rabbits'.

 Start with two overlapping shapes, a circle and a large oval, for the rabbit's distinctive body shape. Add a smaller circle sitting on top of the first one for the head.

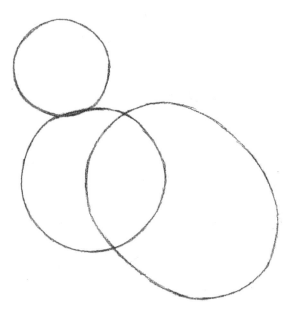

2 Draw two large teardrop shapes for the ears. Then add the legs as simple shapes, the front legs sitting underneath the body's circle and the hind legs a long way back under the oval.

3 Draw two oval shapes in front of the head for the muzzle, with a nose in between. Join the ears to the head and mark in the eye. Shape the back end, adding a little tail.

4 Work on the outline details around the head and eye. Draw some individual toes on the feet.

THUMPING AND HOPPING

In the wild, rabbits are food for animals such as foxes and birds of prey. They warn other rabbits of danger by thumping their powerful hind legs on the ground. If necessary, they hop away in zig-zags to try to confuse and outwit their attacker.

ANIMAL FACTS

5 Now work over the whole drawing to make the rabbit look as soft and friendly as you can. I chose to give mine bold black and white markings, so I drew the outlines of the black patches to guide me at the inking stage.

6 Although this rabbit has patches of solid black, I did not want to use ink for all of these areas because this would make for a flat and lifeless picture. I reserved the black ink for the very darkest parts, and for some delicate outlines around the rest of the animal.

7 For the delicate shading I used a brown-blue mix, which is less dull than plain grey. I built up the shade in two or three layers, using light marks. For the black, I used a mix of very dark blue and dark red. I built up the black with several layers, blending it into the black ink patches. Some spots of pink and yellow-brown added detail to the feet, ears and nose. For a few highlights on the fur, I used diluted white ink.

You can build on the skills you have learned in this book by putting your favourite pets into a scene. Here I have chosen the cat and the dog.

 1 After playing around with various ideas on scrap paper, I settled on this **composition**. I decided to stand the cat on a raised surface, and to make the animals appear to be looking at each other. I reworked it, still at a small scale. Doing rough versions like this can save a lot of time later.

2 I decided that my pencil rough looked a little unbalanced, so I added a rail on the left-hand side of the picture. Then I roughly applied shade and colour with watercolours. I restricted my palette to greens and yellowy browns, with some touches of blue here and there.

 3 Once I was happy with the colouring, I went on to develop the light and shade. Then I used black and white ink to strengthen the outlines and highlights. In this small rough I have established the main areas of light and shade which will help with the larger-scale artwork.

On a large sheet of good paper, sketch in the guidelines for the final artwork. The aim here is to establish a loose framework for all the different parts of the picture – the lines of the decking and fencing, and the rough shapes of the animals.

 With the framework and positions established, you can now develop the shapes, avoiding too much detail until all the necessary guidelines are in place.

6 With a fine pencil and eraser, work over all the important details, erasing any confusing guidelines as you go. I left the fine detail that I would need for the next (inking) stage.

7 I used dark brown ink to avoid the outlines being too harsh. I watered it down to outline distant and less important features. For the dog, I used a golden brown ink. Once the ink was dry, I erased all the pencil work.

8 Using my colour rough as a guide, I painted in the shadows and shading using purple-brown and blue-green. Then I added in the colours, leaving no white paper showing. I strengthened some of the colours as necessary, before adding highlights. I also mixed white with different greens to add texture to some of the plants.

GLOSSARY

angular Describes something with bends and corners (angles).

composition The arrangement of the different parts of a picture.

muzzle The nose and mouth of an animal such as a cat or dog.

proportion The size of one thing in relation to another.

rodent A mammal such as a mouse, rat or squirrel that has teeth adapted for gnawing and nibbling.

rump The back part of an animal.

symmetrical Describes something that is the same on both sides of a centre point or line.

WEBSITES

http://a-z-animals.com/
An online animal encyclopedia, complete with quizzes and games.

http://www.bbc.co.uk/newsround/animals/
Animal news from around the world.

FURTHER READING

Art Ideas: Drawing Animals by Anna Milbourne (Usborne Publishing, 2009)

Drawing is Fun: Drawing Pets and Farm Animals by Trevor Cook, Lisa Miles and Rebecca Clunes (Franklin Watts, 2012)

How to Draw Pets by Mark Bergin (Book House, 2011)

INDEX